Introduction To MPEG

MPEG-1, MPEG-2 and MPEG-4

Lawrence Harte

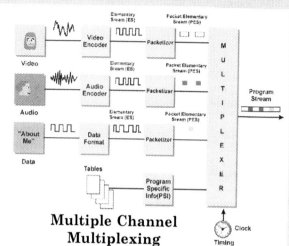

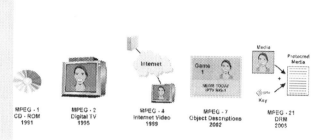

MPEG Evolution

Multiple Channel Multiplexing

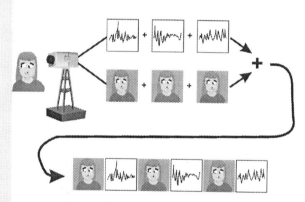

Interlaced Audio and Video

	MPEG-2	MPEG-4/AVC or VC-1
Standard Definition (SD)	3.8 Mbps	1.8 Mbps
High Definition (HD)	19 Mbps	6-8 Mbps

MPEG Video Codec Comparison

Excerpted From:

IPTV Basics

With Updated Information

ALTHOS

ALTHOS Publishing

ALTHOS Publishing

ALTHOS electronic books (ebooks) and images are available for use in educational, promotional materials, training programs, and other uses. For more information about using ALTHOS ebooks and images, please contact April Wiblitzhouser awiblitzhouser@Althos.com or (919) 557-2260.

Terms of Use

About the Author

 Mr. Harte is the president of Althos, an expert information provider whom researches, trains, and publishes on technology and business industries. He has over 29 years of technology analysis, development, implementation, and business management experience. Mr. Harte has worked for leading companies including Ericsson/General Electric, Audiovox/Toshiba and Westinghouse and has consulted for hundreds of other companies. Mr. Harte continually researches, analyzes, and tests new communication technologies, applications, and services. He has authored over 60 books on telecommunications technologies and business systems covering topics such as mobile telephone systems, data communications, voice over data networks, broadband, prepaid services, billing systems, sales, and Internet marketing. Mr. Harte holds many degrees and certificates including an Executive MBA from Wake Forest University (1995) and a BSET from the University of the State of New York, (1990).

Table of Contents

Introduction to MPEG

Motion picture experts group (MPEG) standards are digital video encoding processes that coordinate the transmission of multiple forms of media (multimedia). MPEG is a working committee that defines and develops industry standards for digital video systems. These standards specify the data compression and decompression processes and how they are delivered on digital broadcast systems. MPEG is part of International Standards Organization (ISO).

The MPEG system defines the components (such as a media stream or channel) of a multimedia signal (such as a digital television channel) and how these channels are combined, transmitted, received, separated, synchronized and converted (rendered) back into a multimedia format.

The basic components of a MPEG system include elementary streams (the raw audio, data or video media), program streams (a group of elementary streams that make up a program) and transport streams that carry multiple programs.

Figure 1.1 shows the basic operation of an MPEG system. This diagram shows that the MPEG system allow multiple media types to be used (voice, audio and data), codes and compresses each media type, adds timing information and combines (multiplexes) the media channels into a MPEG program stream. This example shows that multiple program streams (e.g. television programs) can be combined into a transport channel. When the MPEG signal is received, the program channels are separated (demultiplexed), individual media channels are decoded and decompressed and they are converted back into their original media form.

The MPEG system has dramatically evolved since 1991 when it was introduced primarily for use on compact disk (CD) stored media. The first version of MPEG, MPEG-1, was designed for slow speed stored media with moderate computer processing capabilities.

The next evolution of MPEG was MPEG-2, which allowed television broadcasters (such as television broadcasters, cable television and satellite television providers) to convert their analog systems into more efficient and feature rich digital television systems.

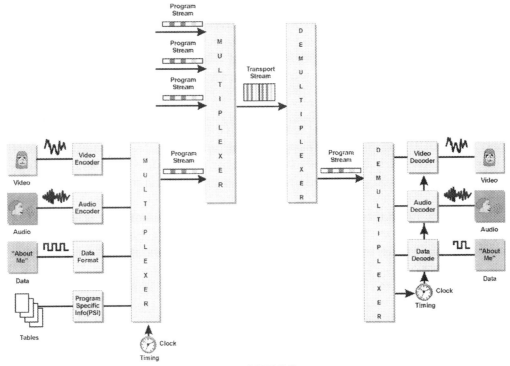

Figure 1.1., MPEG System

Since its introduction, the MPEG-2 system has evolved through the use of extensions to provide new capabilities. The term MPEG-2.5 is a term commonly used to describe an interim generation of MPEG technology that provides more services and features than MPEG-2 but less than the MPEG-4.

The development of an MPEG-3 specification was skipped. MPEG-3 was supposed to be created to enhance MPEG-2 to offer high definition television (HDTV). Because HDTV capability was possible using the MPEG-2 system, MPEG-3 was not released.

The next progression of MPEG technology was the release of the initial parts of the MPEG-4 specification. The MPEG-4 specification allows for television transmission over packet data networks such as broadband internet. The initial release of the MPEG-4 system did not offer much improvement over the MPEG-2 video compression system.

To develop this more efficient video compression technology for MPEG-4, a joint video committee was created. This joint video committee was composed of members from the IETC and ITU for the purpose of analyzing, recommending, solving technical issues to create an advanced video compression specification. The result of this joint effort was the production of the advanced video coder (AVC) that provides standard definition (SD) quality at approximately 2 Mbps. This new part of MPEG-4 video compression (part 10) technology is approximately 50% more efficient (higher compression ratio) than MPEG-2 video coders. The version of AVC defined by the ITU is called H.264.

Figure 1.2 shows how the video coding developed for MPEG-4 was a joint effort between the ISO/IEC and United Nations ITU. Both groups worked together to produce the video coding standard. The ISO/IEC version is called advanced video coding (AVC) and the ITU version is called H.264.

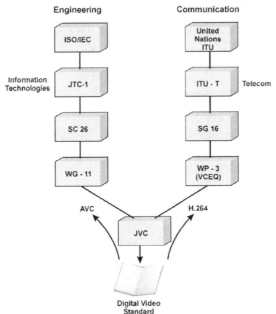

Figure 1.2., MPEG Joint Video Committee

There are other MPEG industry standards including MPEG-7, which is adds descriptions to multimedia objects and MPEG-21, which adds rights management capability to MPEG systems.

Figure 1.3 shows how MPEG systems have evolved over time. This diagram shows that the original MPEG specification (MPEG-1) developed in 1991 offered medium quality digital video and audio at up to 1.2 Mbps, primarily sent via CD ROMs. This standard evolved in 1995 to become MPEG-2, which was used for satellite and cable digital television along with DVD distribution. The MPEG specification then evolved into MPEG-4 in 1999 to permit multimedia distribution through the Internet. This example shows that work continues with MPEG-7 for object based multimedia and MPEG-21 for digital rights management.

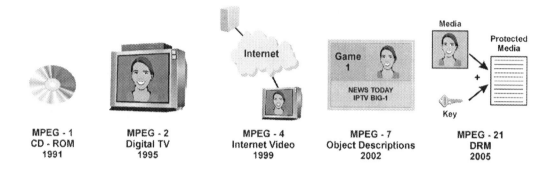

Figure 1.3., MPEG Evolution

Digital Audio

Digital audio is the representation of audio information in digital (discrete level) formats. The use of digital audio allows for more simple storage, processing, and transmission of audio signals. MPEG systems can transfer several channels of digital audio.

Because audio information is in a continuous analog form, analog audio signals are converted to digital (digitized) to allow them to be more processed and transmitted through digital networks (such as the Internet).

To convert analog audio signals to digital form, the analog signal is digitized by using an analog-to-digital (pronounced A to D) converter. The A/D converter periodically senses (samples) the level of the analog signal and creates a binary number or series of digital pulses that represent the level of the signal. The typical sampling rate for conversion of analog audio signals ranges from 8,000 samples per second (for telephone quality) to 44,000 samples per second (for music quality).

Figure 1.4 shows the basic audio digitization process. This diagram shows that a person creates sound pressure waves when they talk. These sound pressure waves are converted to electrical signals by a microphone. The bigger the sound pressure wave (the louder the audio), the larger the analog signal. To convert the analog signal to digital form, the analog signal is periodically sampled and converted to a number of pulses. The higher the level of the analog signal, the larger the number of pulses are created. The number of pulses can be counted and sent as digital numbers. This example also shows that when the digital information is sent, the effects of distortion can be eliminated by only looking for high or low levels. This conversion process is called regeneration or repeating. The regeneration progress allows digital signals to be sent at great distances without losing the quality of the audio sound.

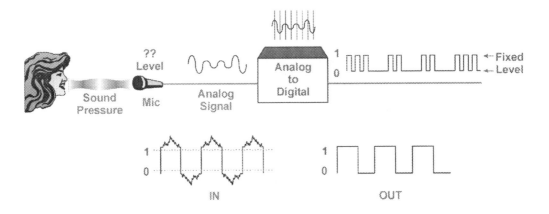

Figure 1.4., Digital Audio

When audio signals are digitized, the amount of raw digital data that is produced can be large. This presents a disadvantage and limitation when storing or transferring the raw data signals. To overcome this challenge, audio compression is used.

Audio compression is a technique for converting or encoding information so that smaller amount of information elements can be used to represent the audio signal. This allows a reduced amount of bits or lower data transmission rate to store transfer digital audio signals.

A sound system may use one (mono) or several audio signals (stereo or surround sound). Stereo is the generation and reproduction of a 2-channel sound source. Stereo signals may be transmitted through the use of independent channels or be sent by sending a single (mono) channel along with difference signal(s). Sound reproduction that surrounds the listener with sound, as in quadraphonic recording has 4 channels. Additional audio channels include a center channel and a sub audio (very low frequency) channel. The MPEG system has the capability to send one or multiple audio channels along with other media (such as audio and video).

Figure 1.5 shows how MPEG allows multiple channels of audio. This example shows that MPEG audio may include left channel, right channel, center channel, left channel surround sound and right channel surround sound. Each of these audio channels are digitized and coded using either level 1 (low complexity), level 2 (medium complexity MUSICAM) or level 3 (high complexity MP3) coding. These channels are combined and multiplexed onto MPEG transport packets. When they are received, they are separated, decoded, and converted from digital back into their original analog form.

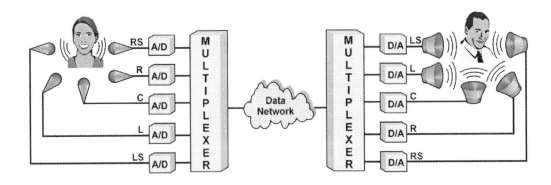

Figure 1.5., MPEG Audio

Digital Video

Digital video is a sequence of picture signals (frames) that are represented by binary data (bits) that describe a finite set of luminance (brightness) and chrominance (color) levels. Sending a digital video sequence involves the conversion of a sequence of images to digital information (e.g. through the use of image scanning) that is transferred to a digital video receiver. The digital information contains characteristics of the video signal and the position of the image that will be displayed. The formats of digital video can vary and the MPEG systems are designed to carry various forms of digital video.

Video images are composed of image elements (pixels) that contain brightness (intensity) and color (chrominance) information. Intensity or luminance is the amount of visible optical energy (intensity) and is measured in Lumens. Chrominance is the portion of the video signal that contains the color information (hue and saturation).

Video signals can be converted into digital form by either converting the combined (composite) analog video signal (intensity and chrominance levels) or by representing each image (frame) of the video by its digital pixel elements. There are several ways that digital images and video may be processed (such as progressively sending images or interlacing adjacent images). The MPEG system was designed to allow the transmission of several different digital video formats.

Figure 1.6 shows a basic process that may be used to digitize images for pictures and video. For color images, each line of image is divided (filtered) into its color components (red, green and blue components). Each position on filtered image is scanned or sampled and converted to a level. Each sampled level is converted into a digital signal.

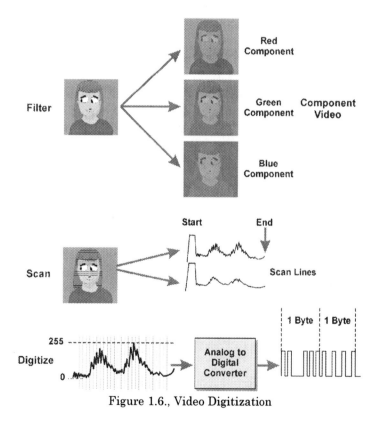

Figure 1.6., Video Digitization

Distribution Systems

Distribution systems are the equipment, software, and interconnecting lines that are used to transfer information to users. MPEG media may be distributed through a variety of types of distribution systems including stored media (such as CD ROMs or DVDs), land based (terrestrial) television broadcast, cable television, satellite transmission or through wired or mobile packet data networks. The characteristics of these types of distribution systems vary and this requires the MPEG system to use different options to ensure the viewer obtains the media with reliable and expected characteristics.

The original MPEG system (MPEG-1) was first developed for stored media (CD ROMs) distribution systems. This type of distribution system provides for relatively high and stable transmission rates with minimum delays and low amounts of errors.

The next version of MPEG (MPEG-2) was designed for broadcast distribution systems. Broadcast systems can provide continuous high data transmission rates with small amounts of delay and low bit error rates (called Quasi error free). Examples of broadcast systems include cable systems, satellite systems and digital terrestrial television (e.g. DVB).

MPEG then evolved to provide television signals over packet data broadcast distribution systems (MPEG-4). Packet broadcast systems often provide variable data transmission rates with varying amounts of delay. Packet broadcast channels can sometimes experience high bit error rates. Examples of packet broadcast systems include broadband television (Internet television) and mobile video.

Figure 1.7 shows some of the types of distribution systems that are used to transfer MPEG. This example shows that MPEG media may be delivered on systems that range from high bandwidth, low error rate stored media systems (e.g. CD ROM) to limited bandwidth, high error rate mobile video. MPEG-1 was designed for stable error free stored media such as CD ROMs. Stored media systems have high-transfer rates and very low error rates. MPEG-2 was developed to allow transmission over broadcast networks such as satellite systems, digital terrestrial television (DTT) and cable television systems. These broadcast systems have some errors and small delays. The MPEG-4 system was developed to allow transmission over packet data networks such as the Internet. These packet data systems usually have variable data transmission rates, unpredictable delays and may experience significant amounts of burst error rates.

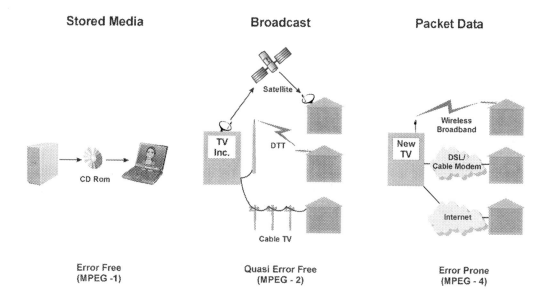

Figure 1.7., MPEG Distribution Systems

Audio Compression

Audio compression is the processing of digital information to a form that reduces the space required for transmission or storage. Audio compression coders and decoders (codecs) analyze digital audio signals to remove signal redundancies and sounds that cannot be heard by humans.

Digital audio data is random in nature unlike digital video which has repetitive information that occurs on adjacent image frames. This means that audio signals do not have a high amount of redundancy, making traditional data compression and prediction processes ineffective at compressing digital audio. It is possible to highly compress digital audio by removing sounds that can be heard or perceived by listeners through the process of perceptual coding.

The type of coder (type of analysis and compression) can dramatically vary and different types of coders may perform better for different types of audio sounds (e.g. speech audio as compared to music). Two key types of audio coders include waveform coders and audio/voice coders.

Waveform coding consists of an analog to digital converter and a data compression circuit that converts analog waveform signal into digital signals that represent the waveform shapes. Waveform coders are capable of compressing and decompressing voice audio, music and other complex signals such as fax or modem signals.

Perceptual coding is the process of converting information into a format that matches the human senses ability to perceive or capture the information. Perceptual coding can take an advantage of the inability of human senses to capture specific types of information. For example, the human ear cannot simultaneously hear loud sounds at one tone (frequency) and soft sounds at another tone (different frequency). Using perceptual coding, it would not be necessary to send signals that cannot be heard even if the original signal contained multiple audio components.

A voice coder is a digital compression device that consists of a speech analyzer that converts analog speech into its component parts, digital signals and speech synthesizer for the recreation of audio signals from the component parts. Voice coders are only capable of compressing and decompressing voice audio signals.

The type of audio coder, its analysis functions, and the data transmission rate determine the quality of the audio and how much complexity (signal processing) that is required for the audio signal. To gain an increased amount of compression, additional signal analysis and processing is usually required. Higher compression typically results in an increase in the complexity of the coding device. Higher complexity (increased signal processing) generally increases the cost and power consumption of the coding device.

The data transmission rate for a compressed audio signal is determined by the audio sampling rate, amount of bits per sample, the compression process used and the parameters selected for the compression process. For example, two channels of audio that are sampled at 44,100 samples per second and each sample produces 16 bits of data and raw uncompressed digital audio at 1.41 Mbps.

The sampling rate and conversion is a key factor in determining the audio quality or fidelity of the audio signal. Audio fidelity is the degree to which a system or a portion of a system accurately reproduces at its output the essential characteristics of the signal impressed upon its input.

The sampling rate of an audio signal is typically performed at least 2x the highest frequency contained within the audio signal. This means if you want to convert an audio signal with a frequency range up to 10 kHz, a sampling rate of at least 20 ksamples per second is required.

The process of audio coding results in delays in the transmission of the digital audio signal and different types of audio coders (different processing techniques) require varying amounts of time for analysis and compression. Typically, there is a tradeoff between perceptual coding and processing delay. Increasing the amount of perceptual coding (higher compression) increases the amount of time it takes to process the signal (processing delay). Some types of audio coders are designed and configured for applications that require low transmission delays (such as real time communication).

Because audio coders compress information or data into codes and codes represent tones or other audio attributes, small errors that occur during transmission can produce dramatically different sounds. As a result, errors that occur on some of the audio data bits (e.g. high volume levels or key frequency tones) can be more sensitive to the listener than errors that occur on other data bits. In some cases, error protection bits may be added to the more significant bits of the compressed audio stream to maintain the audio quality when errors occur.

Figure 1.8 shows the basic operation of an audio codec. This diagram shows that the audio coding process begins with digitization of audio signals. The next step is to analyze the signal into key parts or segments and to repre-

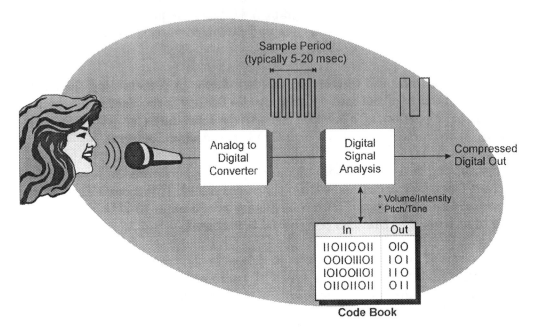

Figure 1.8., Audio Codec Operation

sent the digital audio signal with a compressed code. The compressed code is transmitted to the receiving device that converts the code back into its original audio form.

The MPEG system allows for the use different types of audio coders. The type of coder that is selected can vary based on the application (such as playing music or speech) and the type of device the audio is being played through (such as a television or a battery operated portable media player). The MPEG speech coders range from low complexity (layer 1) to high complexity (layer 3). A new version of audio coder has been created (advanced audio codec-AAC) that offers better audio quality at lower bit rates. The AAC coder also has several variations that are used in different types of applications (e.g. broadcast radio -vs.- real time telephony).

MPEG Layer 1 (MP1)

MPEG layer 1 audio is a low complexity audio compression system. MP1 was the first digital audio and it uses the precision adaptive sub-band coding (PASC) algorithm. This process divides the digital audio signal into multiple frequency bands and only transmits the audio bands that can be heard by the listener. To obtain high fidelity quality (e.g. music) with MP1 typically requires 192 kbps per audio channel.

MPEG Layer 2 (MUSICAM – MP2)

MPEG layer 2 audio is a medium complexity audio compression system which is also known as the MUSICAM system. The MUSICAM system achieves medium compression ratios, dividing the audio signal into sub bands, coding these sub bands and multiplexing them together. The MUSICAM system is used in the (DAB) digital audio broadcasting system. To obtain high fidelity quality (e.g. music) with MP2 typically requires 128 kbps per audio channel.

MPEG Layer 3 (MP3)

MPEG layer 3 is a lossy audio coding standard that uses a relatively high-complexity audio analysis system to characterize and highly compress audio signals. The MP3 system achieves high-compression ratios (10:1 or more) by removing redundant information and sounds that the human ear cannot detect or perceive. The removal of information components that cannot be detected (such as low level signals that occur simultaneously with high-level signals) is called psychoacoustic compression. To obtain high fidelity quality (e.g. music) with MP3 typically requires 64 kbps per audio channel.

The ISO/IEC Moving Picture Experts Group (MPEG) Committee standardized the MP3 codec in 1992. MP3 is intended for high-quality audio (like music) and expert listeners who have found some MP3-encoded audio to be indistinguishable from the original audio at bit rates around 192 kbps. The design of the Layer 3 (MP3) codec was constrained by backward compatibility with the Layer 1 and Layer 2 codecs of the same family.

MPEG Layer 3 Pro (MP3Pro)

MP3Pro is the Motion Picture Experts Group Layer 3 (MP3) system with spectral band replication (SBR) added to improve audio quality and/or lower the necessary data transmission rate.

Advanced Audio Codec (AAC™)

Advanced Audio Codec (AAC) is an audio codec standardized by the ISO/IEC Moving Picture Experts Group (MPEG) Committee in 1997 as an improved but non-backward-compatible alternative to MP3. Like MP3, AAC is intended for high-quality audio (like music) and expert listeners who have found some AAC-encoded audio to be indistinguishable from the original audio at bit rates around 128 kbps, compared with 192 kbps for MP3.

Advanced Audio Codec Plus (AAC Plus™)

Advanced Audio Codec Plus is a version of the AAC coder that is used to provide enhanced audio quality at high frequencies. The AACPlus system uses spectral band replication to improve the audio quality when possible. The AACPlus system has multiple streams of audio information which are composed of a base stream that can be combined with another stream to adjust (improve) the characteristics of the high-frequency audio signal components.

High Efficiency Advanced Audio Codec (HE AAC)

HE ACC is a version of the MPEG AAC system with spectral band replication (SBR) added to improve audio quality and/or lower the necessary data transmission rate.

Advanced Audio Codec Low Delay (AAC LD)

ACC LD is a version of the MPEG AAC system that is designed to provide good audio quality while providing a maximum signal processing delay that does not exceed 20 msec.

Figure 1.9 shows the different types of audio compression used in MPEG systems and the relative amount of compression that they can provide. This table uses a 2 channel stereo signal that is sampled at 44.1k samples per second, 16 bits per sample as a reference. The MPEG layer 1 coder can compress this signal to approximately 384 kbps (4:1 compression). The MPEG layer 2 coder can compress the signal to 192 kbps (8:1 compression). The MP3 coder can compress the signal to 128 kbps (12:1 compression). The AAC coder can compress the signal to 96 kbps (16:1 compression).

	MPEG Layer 1	MPEG Layer 2	MPEG Layer 3 (MP3)	AAC
Raw Data Rate (stereo @ 44.1 ksamples/sec)	1.5 Mbps	1.5 Mbps	1.5 Mbps	1.5 Mbps
Compressed Data Rate	384 kbps	192 kbps	128 kbps	96 kbps
Typical Compression	4:1	8:1	12:1	16:1

Figure 1.9., MPEG Audio Compression Comparison

Video Compression

Video compression is the process of reducing the amount of transmission bandwidth or the data transmission rate by analog processing and/or digital coding techniques. Moving pictures can be compressed by removing redundancy within each image (spatial redundancy) or between successive images over a period of time (temporal redundancy). When compressed, a video signal can be transmitted on circuits with relatively narrow channel bandwidth or using data rates 50 to 200 times lower than their original uncompressed form.

Spatial redundancy is the repetition of information or image elements within an image area. Spatial compression is the analysis and compression of information or data within a single frame, image or section of information. Temporal compression is the analysis and compression of information or data over a sequence of frames, images or sections of information.

Video images are composed of pixels. MPEG system groups pixels within each image into small blocks and these blocks are grouped into macroblocks. Macroblocks can be combined into slices and each image may contain several slices. Slices make up frames, which come in several different types. The different types of frames can be combined into a group of pictures.

Pixels

A pixel is the smallest component in an image. Pixels can range in size and shape and are composed of color (possibly only black on white paper) and intensity. The number of pixels per unit of area is called the resolution. The more pixels per unit area provide more detail in the image.

Blocks

Blocks are portions of an image within a frame of video usually defined by a number of horizontal and vertical pixels. For the MPEG system, each block is composed of 8 by 8 pixels and each block is processed separately.

Macroblocks

A macroblock is a region of a picture in a digital picture sequence (motion pictures) that may be used to determine motion compensation from a reference frame to other pictures in a sequence of images. Typically, a frame is divided into 16 by 16 pixel sized macroblocks, which is also groupings of four 8 by 8-pixel blocks.

Slice

A slice is a part of an image that is used in digital video and it is composed of a contiguous group of macroblocks. Slices can vary in size and shape.

Frames

A frame is a single still image within the sequence of images that comprise the video. In an interlaced scanning video system, a frame comprises two fields. Each field contains half of the video scan lines that make up the picture, the first field typically containing the odd numbered scan lines and the second field typically containing the even numbered scan lines.

To compress video signals, the MPEG system categorizes video images (frames) into different formats. These formats vary from fame types that only use spatial compression (independently compressed) to frames that use both spatial compression and temporal compression (predicted frames).

MPEG system frame types include independent reference frames (I-frames), predicted frames that are based on previous reference frames (P-frames), bi-directionally predicted frames using preceding frames and frames that follow (B-Frames), and DC frames (basic block reference levels).

Intra Frames (I-Frames)

Intra frames (I-Frames) are complete images (pictures) within a sequence of images (such as in a video sequence). I-frames are used as a reference for other compressed image frames and I frames are completely independent of other frames. The only redundancy that can be removed from I frames is spatial redundancy. This means that I-frames require more data than compressed frames.

Predicted Frames (P-Frames)

Predicted frames (P-Frames) are images (pictures) within a sequence of images (such as in a video sequence) that are created using information from other images (such as from Intra Frames (I-Frames).

Because image components are often repeated within a sequence of images (temporal redundancy), the use of P-Frames provides substantial reduction in the number of bits that are used to represent a digital video sequence (temporal data compression).

Bi-Directional Frames (B-Frames)

Bidirectional frames (B-Frames) are images (pictures) within a sequence of images (such as in a video sequence) that are created using information from preceding images, images that follow (such as from intra frames (I-Frames) and predicted frames (P-Frames).

Because B-Frames are created using both preceding images and images that follow, B-frames offer more data compression capability than P-Frames. B-frames require the use of frames that both precede and follow the B-frames. Because B frames must be compared to two other frames, the amount of image processing that is required for B-frames (e.g. motion estimation) is typically higher than P frames.

DC Frames (D-Frames)

A DC frame is an image in a motion video sequence that represents the DC level of the image. D frames are used in the MPEG-1 system to allow rapid viewing (e.g. fast forwarding) and are not used in other versions of MPEG.

Groups of Pictures (GOP)

Frames can be grouped into sequences called a group of pictures (GOP). A GOP is an encoding of a sequence of frames that contain all the information that can be completely decoded within that GOP. For all frames within a GOP that reference other frames (such as B-frames and P-frames), the frames so referenced (I-frames and P-frames) are also included within that same GOP.

The types of frames and their location within a GOP can be defined in time (temporal) sequence. The temporal distance of images is the time or number of images between specific types of images in a digital video. M is the distance between successive P-Frames and N is the distance between successive I-Frames. Typical values for MPEG GOP are M equals 3 and N equals 12.

Figure 1.10 shows how different types of frames can compose a group of pictures (GOP). A GOP can be characterized as the depth of compressed predicted frames (m) as compared to the total number of frames (n). This example shows that a GOP starts within an intra-frame (I-frame) and that intra-frames typically requires the largest number of bytes to represent the image (200 kB in this example). The depth m represents the number of frames that exist between the I-frames and P-frames.

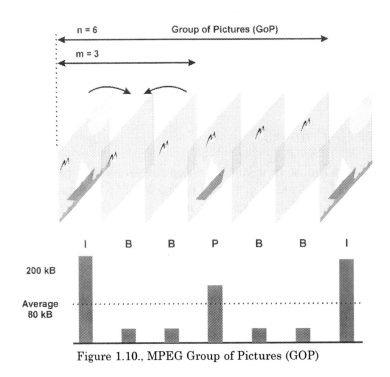

Figure 1.10., MPEG Group of Pictures (GOP)

Groups of pictures can be independent (closed) GOP or they can be relative (open) to other GOPs. An open group of pictures is a sequence of image frames that requires information from other GOPs to successfully decode all the frames within its sequence. A closed group of pictures is a sequence of image frames can successfully decode all the frames within its sequence without using information from other GOPs.

Because P and B frames are created using other frames, when errors occur on previous frames, the error may propagate through additional frames (error retention). To overcome the challenge of error propagation, I frames are sent periodically to refresh the images and remove and existing error blocks.

Figure 1.11 shows how errors that occur in an MPEG image may be retained in frames that follow. This example shows how errors in a B-Frame are transferred to frames that follow as the B-Frame images are created from preceding images.

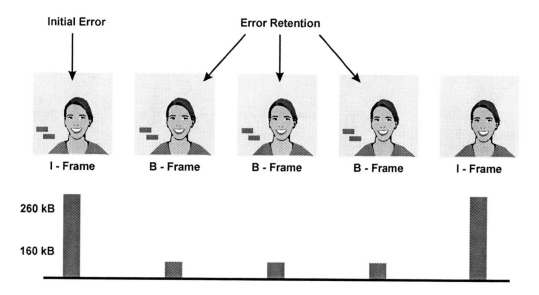

Figure 1.11., MPEG Error Retention

Motion Estimation

Motion estimation is the process of searching a fixed region of a previous frame of video to find a matching block of pixels of the same size under consideration in the current frame. The process involves an exhaustive search for many blocks surrounding the current block from the previous frame. Motion estimation is a computer-intensive process that is used to achieve high compression ratios.

Figure 1.12 shows how a digital video system can use motion estimation to identify objects and how their positions change in a series of pictures. This diagram shows that a bird in a picture is flying across the picture. In each picture frame, the motion estimation system looks for blocks that approximate other blocks in previous pictures. Over time, the digital video motion estimation system finds matches and determines the paths (motion vectors) that these objects take.

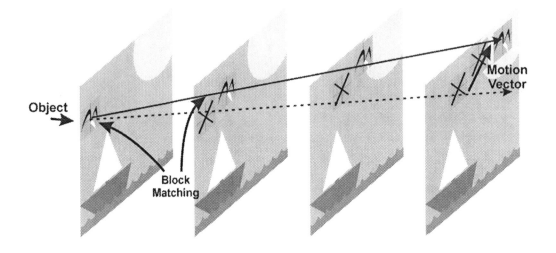

Figure 1.12., MPEG Motion Estimation

Compression Scalability

Compression scalability is the ability of a media compression system to adapt its compression parameters for various conditions such as display size (spatial scalability), combining multiple transmission channels (layered scalability), changing the frame rate (temporal scalability) or quality of signal (signal to noise scalability).

Spatial scalability is the ability of a media file or picture image to reduce or vary the number of image components or data elements representing a picture over a given area (spatial area) without significantly changing the quality or resolution of the image.

Layered scalability is the use of multiple layers in an image that can be combined to produce higher resolution images or video. Layered compression starts with the use of a base layer may be decoded separately to provide a low resolution preview of the image or video and to reduce the decoding processing requirements (reduced complexity). An enhancement layer is a stream or source of media information that is used to improve (enhance) the resolution or appearance of underlying image (e.g. base layers).

Temporal scalability is the ability of a streaming media program or moving picture file to reduce or vary the number of images or data elements representing that media file for a particular time period (temporal segment) without significantly changing the quality or resolution of the media over time.

Signal to noise ratio scalability is the ability of a media file or picture image to reduce or vary the number of image components or data elements representing that that picture to compensate for changes in the signal to noise ratio of the transport signal.

Advanced Video Coding (AVC/H.264)

Advanced video coding is a video codec that can be used in the MPEG-4 standard. The AVC coder provides standard definition (SD) quality at approximately 2 Mbps and high definition (HD) quality at approximately 6-8 Mbps.

The AVC coding system achieves higher compression ratios by better analysis and compression of the underlying media. The AVC system can identify and separately code objects from video sequences (object coding), it can create or represent objects in synthetic form (animated objects) and it can use variable block sizes to more efficiently represent (deblock) images with varying edges.

Object Coding

Object coding is the representation of objects (such as a graphic item in a frame of video) through the use of a code or character sequence. The types of objects that can be used in AVC system range from static background images (sprites) to synthetic video (animation).

A background sprite is a graphic object that is located behind foreground objects. Background sprites usually don't change or they change relatively slowly. Audiovisual objects are parts of media images (media elements). Media images or moving pictures may be analyzed and divided into audiovisual objects to allow for improved media compression or audiovisual objects may be combined to form new images or media programs (synthetic video).

Media elements are component parts of media images or content programs. A media element can be the smallest common denominator of an image or media program component. A media element is considered a unique specific element such as a shape, texture and size.

Animated Objects

Animated objects are graphic elements that can be created and changed over a period of time. Animated objects can be used to create synthetic video (e.g. moving picture information that is created through the use creating image components by non-photographic means).

MPEG-4 uses an efficient form (a binary form) of virtual reality modeling language (VRML) to create 3 dimensional images. This allows the MPEG system to send a mathematical model of objects along with their associated textures instead of sending detailed images that require large data transmission bandwidths.

Variable Block Sizes

Variable block sizes are groups of image bits that make up a portion of an image that vary in width and height. The use of variable block sizes allows for using smaller blocks in portions of graphic images that have lots of rapid variations (such as the edge of a sharp curve). Also, it allows larger blocks in areas that have a limited amount of variation (such as the solid blue portion of the sky).

Figure 1.13 shows comparison of MPEG-2 and the new MPEG-4/AVC video coding system. This diagram shows that the standard MPEG-2 video compression system requires approximately 3.8 Mbps for standard definition (SD) television and 19 Mbps for high definition (HD) television. The MPEG-4 AVC video coding system requires approximately 1.8 Mbps for SD television and 6 to 8 Mbps for HD television.

	MPEG-2	MPEG-4/AVC or VC-1
Standard Definition (SD)	3.8 Mbps	1.8 Mbps
High Definition (HD)	19 Mbps	6-8 Mbps

Figure 1.13., Video Codec Operation

Media Streams

A media stream is a flow of information that represents a media signal (such as digital audio or digital video). A media stream may be continuous (circuit based) or bursty (packetized). MPEG systems are composed of various types of streams ranging from the basic raw data stream (elementary streams) to stream that contain a single television video (a program stream) or a stream that combines multiple programs (transport streams).

The key elements to streaming in the MPEG system include combining multiple packet streams into a single program or transport stream, to add the time reference information into the streams and to manage the buffers required to receive and process the elementary streams.

Figure 1.14 shows the basic process of streaming video programs through a packet data network. This diagram shows that media streaming involves converting media into a stream of packets, periodically inserting time references and controlling temporary buffer sizes. .

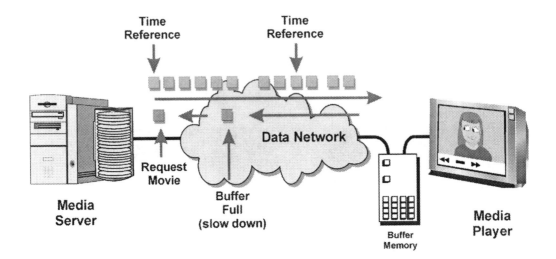

Figure 1.14., Media Streaming

Elementary Stream (ES)

Elementary streams are the raw information component streams (such as audio and video) that are part of a program stream. MPEG system divides a multimedia source component into an elementary stream (ES). Elementary streams may be video, audio or data and there may be several elementary streams for each type of media (such as multiple audio channels for surround sound).

Packet Elementary Stream (PES)

A packet elementary stream is a raw information component stream (such as audio and video) that has been converted to packet form (a sequence of packets). This packetization process involves dividing (segmenting) a group of bits in an elementary stream and adding packet header information to the data. This packet header includes a packet identification code (PID) that uniquely identifies the packetized elementary stream from all other packetized elementary streams that are transmitted. PES packets are variable length packets that have a length limited determined by 16 bits length field in the header of each packet.

PES streams may include time decoding and presentation time stamps that help the receiver to decode and present the media. Decoding time stamps are the insertion of reference timing information that indicates when the decoding of a packet or stream of data should occur. A presentation time stamp is reference timing values that are included in MPEG packet media streams (digital audio, video or data) that are used to control the presentation time alignment of media.

Program Stream (PS)

A program stream is a combination of elementary streams (such as video and audio) that compose a media program (such as a television program). A program stream is called single program transport stream (SPTS). All the packets in a program stream must share the same time reference system time clock (STC).

The packet size for program streams can have different lengths. For media distribution systems that have a low error rate, longer packets may be used. For media distribution systems that have medium to high error rates (such as radio transmission or Internet systems), shorter packet lengths are typically used.

Transport Stream (TS)

Transport Streams are the combining (multiplexing) of multiple program channels (typically digital video channels) onto a signal communication channel (such as a satellite transponder channel). A MPEG transport stream (MPEG-TS) is also called a multi-program transport stream (MPTS).

MPEG transport streams (MPEG-TS) use a fixed length packet size and a packet identifier identifies each transport packet within the transport stream. A packet identifier in an MPEG system identifies the packetized elementary streams (PES) of a program channel. A program (such as a television show) is usually composed of multiple PES channels (e.g. video and audio).

Because MPEG-TS carry multiple programs, to identify the programs carried on a MPEG-TS, a program allocation table and program mapping table is periodically transmitted which provides a list of the programs contained within the MPEG-TS. These program tables provide a list of programs and their associated PIDs for specific programs which allows the MPEG receiver/decoder to select and decode the correct packets for that specific program.

MPEG transport packets are a fixed size of 188 bytes with a 4 byte header. The payload portion of the MPEG-TS packet is 184 bytes. The beginning of a transport packet includes a synchronization byte that allows the receiver to determine the exact start time of the packet. This is followed by an error indication (EI) bit that identifies there was an error in a previous transmission process. A payload unit start indicator (PUSI) flag alerts the receiver if the packet contains the beginning (start) of a new PES. The transport priority indicator identifies if the packet has low or high priority. The 13 bit packet identifier (PID) is used to define which PES is contained in the packet. The scrambling control flag identifies if the data is encrypted. An adaptation field control defines if an adaptation field is used in the payload of the transport packet and a continuity counter maintains a count index between sequential packets.

Figure 1.15 shows an MPEG transport stream and a transport packet structure. This diagram shows that an MPEG-TS packet is fixed size of 188 bytes including a 4-byte header. The header contains various fields including an initial synchronization (time alignment) field, flow control bits, packet identifier (which PES stream is contained in the payload) and additional format and flow control bits.

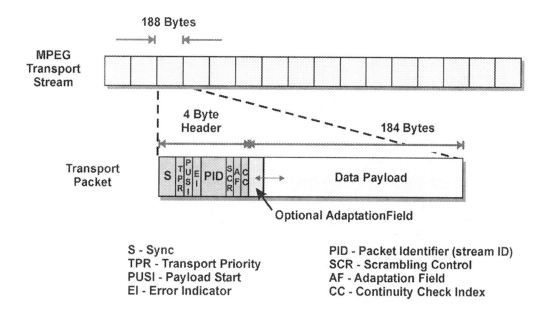

Figure 1.15., MPEG Transport Stream (MPEG-TS) Packet

PES packets tend to be much longer than transport packets. This requires that the PES packets be divided into segments so they can fit into the 184-byte payload of a transport packet. Each packet in the transport stream only contains data from a single PES. Because the division of PES packets into 184-byte segments will likely result in a remainder portion (segment) that is not exactly 184 bytes, an adaptation field is used to fill the transport packet. An adaptation field is a portion of a data packet or block of data that is used to adjust (define) the length or format of data that is located in the packet or block of data.

Figure 1.16 shows how PES packets are inserted into a MPEG transport stream. This example shows how a video and an audio packet elementary stream may be combined onto an MPEG-TS. This example shows that each of the PES packets is larger than the MPEG transport stream packets. Each PES packet is divided into segments that fit into the transport stream packets.

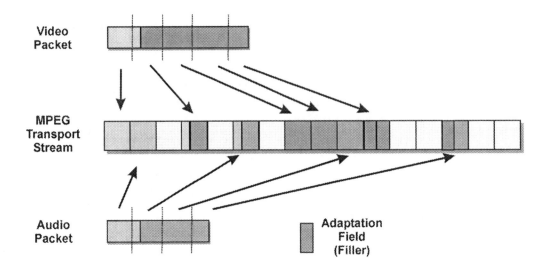

Figure 1.16., Transferring MPEG PES packets into TS Packets

MPEG Transmission

MPEG transmission is the process of combining, sending and managing the transmission of multiple forms of information (multimedia). A program stream is a combination of elementary streams (such as video and audio) that compose a media program (such as a television program).

A mulitprogram transport streams is the combining (multiplexing) of multiple program channels (typically digital video channels) onto a signal communication channel (such as a satellite transponder channel). These channels are statistically combined in such a way that the bursty transmission (high video activity) of one channel is merged with the low-speed data transmission (low video activity) with other channels so more program channels can share the same limited bandwidth communication channel.

This figure shows how MPEG transmission can be used to combine video, audio, and data onto one data communication channel. This example shows that multiple types of media signals are digitized and compressed and sent to a multiplexer. The multiplexer combines these signals and their associated time reference (clock) into a single program transport stream (SPTS). When the SPTS is received, a demultiplexer separates each of the media signal streams. Each media stream is decoded, adjusted in time sequenced using the reference clock and converted back into their original media form.

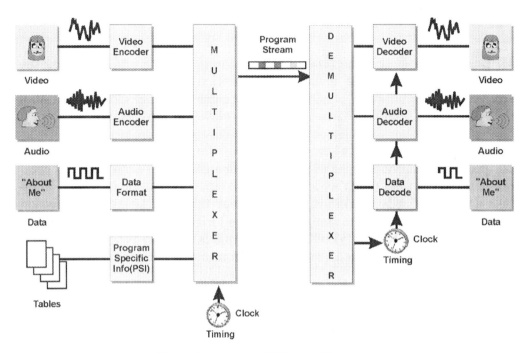

Figure 1.17.., Basic MPEG Multiplexing

Packet Sequencing

Packet sequencing is the process of organizing packets into a sequence that is in a usable format for the system. MPEG packet sequencing from the encoder is not necessarily the same sequence that is required by the decoder. The decoding and presentation times for frames may not be the same because some of the frames may be created from future frames. B frames must be created from P frames and I frames and P frames are created from I frames.

To identify when frames should be presented, time stamps are in inserted. The MPEG system has many types of time stamps including system time stamp (STS), decoding time stamps (DTS) and presentation time stamps (PTS). MPEG system time stamps may be mandatory (such as STS) or optional time stamps (such as DTS and PTS).

Figure 1.18 shows how the encoder packet sequence differs from the decoder packet sequence. This example an encoder that starts providing a video sequence with a reference I frame (1). B frames (2,3) that are created from the I frame (1) and the future P frame (4) follow this. B frames (5,6) that are created follow the P frame (4) and future I frame (7). This diagram shows that because the B frames are created from I frames and P frames, the sequence of packets provided from the decoder are different. The decoder must produce the I frames and P frames before it can produce the B frames. This example shows that the output of the decoder is I frame (1) and P frame (4) which are used to produce B frames (2,3) and P frame (4) and I frame (7) are used to produce B frames (5,6).

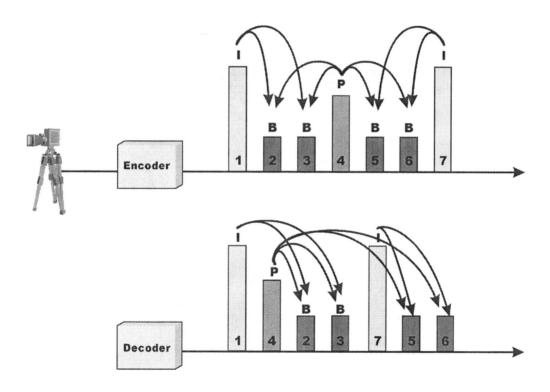

Figure 1.18.., MPEG Packet Sequencing

Packet Routing

Packet routing involves the transmission of packets through intelligent switches (called routers) that analyze the destination address of the packet and determine a path that will help the packet travel towards its destination.

Figure 1.19 shows how blocks of data are divided into small packet sizes that can be sent through the Internet. After the data is divided into packets (envelopes shown in this example), a destination address along with some description about the contents is added to each packet (called in the packet header). As the packet enters into the Internet (routing boxes shown in this diagram), each router reviews the destination address in its routing table and determines which paths it can send the packet to so it will move further towards its destination. If a current path is busy or unavailable (such as shown for packet #3), the router can forward the packets to other routers that can forward the packet towards its destination. This example shows that because some packets will travel through different paths, packets may

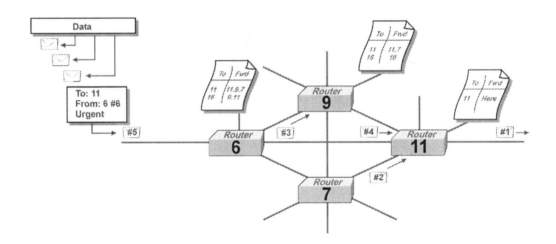

Figure 1.19., Packet Transmission

arrive out of sequence at their destination. When the packets arrive at their destination, they can be reassembled into proper order using the packet sequence number.

Packet delays are a varying amount of time packets take to travel from their source to their destination. Packet delays occur due to the processing time of routers, traffic congestion and the ability of packets to take alternative routes to reach their destination. Packet delays can cause packet jitter.

Packet jitter is the short-term variation of transmission delay time for data packets that usually results from varying time delays in transmission due to different paths or routing processes used in a packet communication network.

Packet loss is a ratio of the number of data packets that have been lost in transmission compared to the total number of packets that have been transmitted.

Figure 1.20 shows how some packets may be lost during transmission through a communications system. This example shows that several packets enter into the Internet. The packets are forwarded toward their destination as usual. Unfortunately, a lighting strike corrupts (distorts) packet 8 and it cannot be forwarded. Packet 6 is lost (discarded) when a router has exceeded its capacity to forward packets because too many were arriving at the same time. This diagram shows that the packets are serialized to allow them to be placed in correct order at the receiving end. When the receiving end determines a packet is missing in the sequence, it can request that another packet be retransmitted. If the time delivery of packets is critical (such as for packetized voice), it is common that packet retransmission requests are not performed and the lost packets simply result in distortion of the received information (such as poor audio quality).

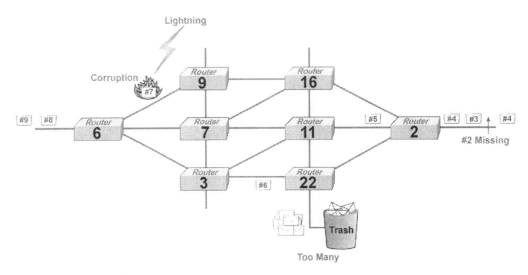

Figure 1.20., Packet Losses

Multicasting

Multicasting is the process of transmitting media channels to a number of users through the use of distributed channels (copying media channels) as they progress through a network. Using multicast medium access control (MAC) or Internet protocol (IP) addresses, multiple end users may "tune" to the same stream of data as it is transmitted over the network. This is in contrast to a unicast transmission whereby multiple copies of the stream, each individually addressed to an end user, are transmitted over the network. Multicasting provides much more efficient use of the network resources, however, individual users are not able to use functions such as pause and fast-forward.

Figure 1.21 shows how a single source multicast data session to allow a single source to send the same information to multiple receivers without the need to repeat the transmission back through multiple switches and routers in the network. This example shows that an IP address source is combined with a single multicast address that allows each router in the multicast tree to forward the packets only to members of the group.

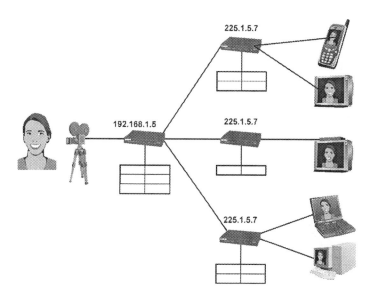

Figure 1.21., Data Multicasting

Channel Multiplexing

Channel multiplexing is a process that divides a single transmission path into several parts that can transfer multiple communication (voice and/or data) channels. Multiplexing may be frequency division (dividing into frequency bands), time division (dividing into time slots), code division (dividing into coded data that randomly overlap), or statistical multiplexing (dynamically assigning portions of channels when activity exists).

A FlexMux is a set of tools that are used by a multimedia system (such as MPEG) that allows for the combining of multiple media sources (such as video and audio) so that the media streams are combined and resynchronized back into its original composite form.

Figure 1.22 shows how MPEG transmission can be used to combine video, audio, and data onto one packet data communication channel. This example shows that multiple types of signals are digitized and converted into a format suitable for the MPEG packetizers. This example shows a MPEG channel that includes video, audio, and user data for a television message. This example shows that each media source is packetized and sent to a multiplexer that combines the channels into a single transport stream. The multiplexer also combines program specific information that describes the content and format of the media channels. The multiplexer uses a clock to time stamp the MPEG information to allow it to be separated and recreated in the correct time sequence.

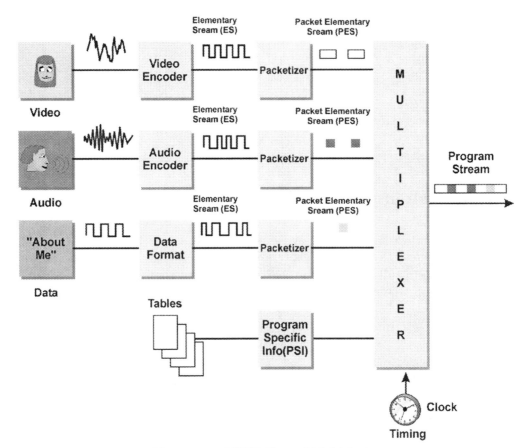

Figure 1.22., MPEG Channel Multiplexing

Statistical Multiplexing

Statistical multiplexing is the process of transferring communication information on an as-needed statistical basis. For statistical multiplexing systems, connections can be initiated and maintained according to anticipated activity need. Each communication channel is dynamically allocated by time slots or codes on a main transmission facility. This allows a communication system to operate more efficiently based by transferring information only when there is activity (such as voice or video signals).

Program channels combined on a MPEG-TS may be statistically combined in such a way that the bursty transmission (high video activity) of one channel is merged with the low-speed data transmission (low video activity) with other channels so more program channels can share the same limited bandwidth communication channel.

A statistical multiplexer can analyze traffic density and dynamically switch to a different channel pattern to speed up the transmission. At the receiving end, the different signals are merged back into individual streams.

Figure 1.23 shows how multiple MPEG channels may be combined using statistical multiplexing to help average the bandwidth usage. This example shows 3 MPEG video channels that have variable bandwidth due to high video activity periods (action scenes with high motion). The combined data rate is shown at the bottom. The combined data rate has a peak data rate that is larger than the 10 Mbps transmission channel can allow. As a result, one or more of the input MPEG channels must use a higher compression rate (temporary lower picture quality).

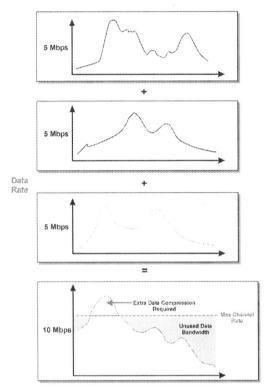

Figure 1.23., MPEG Statistical Multiplexing

MPEG Program Tables

MPEG tables are groups of structured information that describe programs, program components or other information that is related to the delivery and decoding of programs. MPEG tables can be used by electronic programming guides (EPG) to inform the user of the available channels. The EPG is the interface (portal) that allows a customer to preview and select from possible lists of available content media. EPGs can vary from simple program selection to interactive filters that dynamically allow the user to filter through program guides by theme, time period, or other criteria.

There are many types of MPEG program tables and the more common tables contain listings of programs in a transport channel (PAT), program components (video and audio streams) and conditional access information (to enable decryption and decoding).

Program Allocation Table (PAT)

A program allocation table contains the identification codes and system information associated with programs that are contained in a transport stream. The PAT is usually sent every 20 msec to 100 msec to allow the receiver to quickly acquire a list of available programs.

Program Map Table (PMT)

Program map table contains information that identifies and describes the components (such as the video and audio elementary streams) that are parts of a program (such as a television show). Using the PIDs in the PMT, the receiver can select and combine the different media components to recreate the television program.

Conditional Access Table (CAT)

A conditional access table holds information that is used by an access device (such as a set top box with a smart card) to decode programs that are part of a conditional access system (e.g. on-demand programs). If any of the programs have conditional access control, the CAT table transmitted on PID 01. The CAT table provides the packet identifier (PID) channel code that provides the entitlement management messages (EMM) to the descrambler assembly.

Private Tables

Private tables are user defined data elements that are sent along with broadcast programs (such as a television show).

Figure 1.24 shows how the MPEG system uses tables to describe programs and the media streams that are contained within the programs. This diagram shows that a program allocation table (PAT) is typically sent every 20 msec to 100 msec. The PAT provides the information necessary to obtain the program map table (PMT) that a viewer may want to receive. The PMT contains the information necessary to receive and decode a specific program and its media components (elementary streams). If a program has conditional access rights management associated with it, a conditional access table (CAT) will be included in the MPEG program stream. This example shows that the receiver first obtains the PAT (step 1) to obtain the PID of

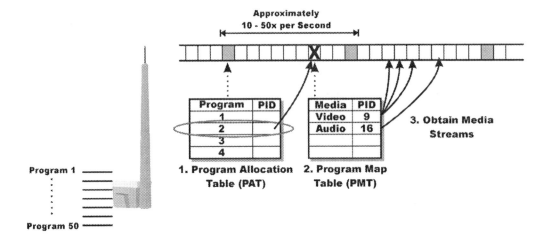

Figure 1.24., MPEG Tables

the PMT. After the receiver has obtained the PMT (step 2), it will use the information in the table to obtain and classify the elementary stream packets (step 3).

Video Modes

Video modes are condition of operation that is used to transfer video images. The MPEG system can represent video images in the form of individual images (frame mode) or interlaced images (field mode).

Because some television media is stored in analog video format that use interlacing, this video must be converted into a format that can be sent on a digital broadcast system. Converting interlaced video may be performed using frame mode (alternating frames), field mode or mixed mode.

Frame Mode

Frame mode is the process of sending video as separate images where each image (a frame) in a sequence of a movie adds a complete image. Frame mode is also known as progressive mode.

Field Mode

Field mode is the process of sending video as images in pairs where each adjacent image (a field) of the pair contains information (image lines) that completes the image in the alternate field. Field mode for MPEG was created to allow for the sending of video that is in interlaced form.

Interlaced video is a sequence of images (video) that uses alternating graphic lines (e.g. odd and even) to represent each picture scan (fields). Analog television systems use interlacing to decrease the bandwidth required (less picture information) and increase the image presentation rate (increased images per second) to reduce flicker effects.

Mixed Mode

Mixed mode is a process of converting interlaced video images (fields) into progressive video images (frames).

Media Flow Control

Media flow control is the hardware and/or software mechanism or protocol that coordinates the transfer of information between devices. Flow control can be used to adjust the transmission rates between devices when one communication device cannot receive the information at the same rate as it is being sent. This can occur when the receiver requires extensive processing and the receiving buffers are running low.

For MPEG systems, media flow control primarily allows for the adjustment of transmission parameters. For one-way systems (such as MPEG-2 broadcast), flow control may be managed by the transmitting end through the use of variable compression rates or for two-way MPEG systems such as MPEG-4, information may be exchanged between the receiver and the transmitter to adjust the data transmission parameters.

Quantizer Scaling

Quantizer scaling is the process of changing the quantizer threshold levels to adjust the data transmission rates from a media encoder. The use of quantizer scaling allows an MPEG system to provide a fixed data transmission rate by adjusting the amount of media compression.

MPEG image blocks are converted into their frequency components through the use of discrete cosine transform (DCT). The DCT converts an image map into its frequency components (from low detail to high detail). Each frequency component converted (quantized) into a specific value (coefficient). The accuracy of each of these quantized values determines how close the image block represents the original image.

Because many of the frequency components hold small values (small amounts of detail), it is possible to reduce the amount of data that represents a block of an image by eliminating the fine details through the use of thresholding. Thresholds are value that must be exceeded for an event to occur or for data to be recorded. Quantizer scaling uses an adjustable threshold level that determines if the level of frequency component should be included in the data or should a 0 level (no information) be transmitted in its place.

Figure 1.25 shows how MPEG system can use quantizer scaling to control the data rate by varying the amount of detail in an image. This example shows that an image is converted into frequency component levels and that each component has a specific level. This example shows that setting the quantizer level determines if the coefficient data will be sent or if a 0 (no data) will be used in its place.

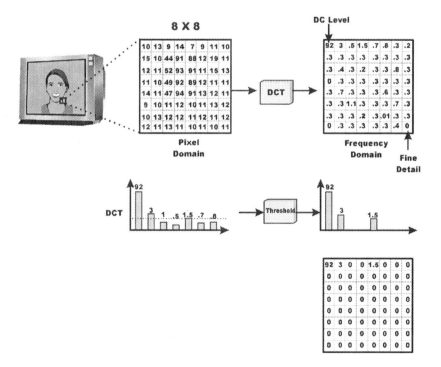

Figure 1.25., MPEG Quantizer Scaling

Bit Rate Control

Bit rate control is a process of setting and/or adjusting the rate of a process or transmission. MPEG systems may use bit rate control to adjust the data rate of a MPEG program to match the specific capabilities or requirements of a transmission line.

When significant amounts of motion (e.g. action scenes) occur in the video, the encoded data transmission rate increases. If the data transmission rate exceeds the available transmission rate, quantizer scaling can be used to reduce the data transmission rate.

Increasing the quantizer threshold level reduces the amount of data that is sent with each block. This also reduces the detail and accuracy of each block that is transmitted. This is why digital television programs can display blockiness during periods of rapid changes in video (e.g. action scenes).

To perform bit rate control, the MPEG transmitter contains a bit rates sensing mechanism. When the bit rate from the digital video encoder starts to exceed the allowable amount (e.g. the maximum data transmission rate of the transmission channel), it increases the quantizer scaling level. The increased quantizer scaling level reduces the detail of the blocks (increased threshold level) and this reduces the data rate. When the data rate starts to decline (e.g. less changes in video), the quantizer scaling can be reduced adding detail back into the digital video.

Figure 1.26 shows how an MPEG system may use quantizer scaling to adjust the data transmission bit rate in an MPEG system. This diagram shows that the MPEG encoder is required to maintain a data transmission rate of 4 Mbps. When the data transmission rate increases, the quantizer-scaling factor is increased to reduce the data transmission rate. The trade-off of higher compression is increased blockiness in the image.

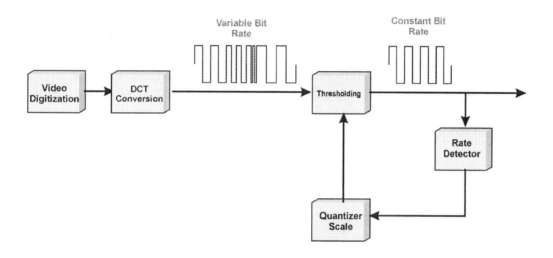

Figure 1.26., MPEG Bit Rate Control

Buffering

Buffering is an allocation of memory storage that set aside for temporary storage of data. The use of memory buffers allows data transfer rates to vary so that differences in communication speeds between devices do not interrupt normal processing operations.

The use of buffering allows for variations in the data rate of the digital video while maintaining a constant data transmission rate. The MPEG system has the capability to setup and manage the size of buffers in receivers to allow for variation in data transmission rates.

Figure 1.27 shows how packet buffering can be used in MPEG systems to allow for some variations in digital video rates. This diagram shows that during the conversion of a digital video signal to an MPEG format, the data rate varies. Because this MPEG system has a buffer, some of the data from time periods of high video activity can be deferred into time periods of low activity. During periods of high video activity, data from the buffer is consumed at a faster rate than the transmission line can provide which results in the buffer levels decreasing. During periods of low video activity, the data from the buffer is consumed at a slower rate than the transmission line can provide allowing the buffer level to increase.

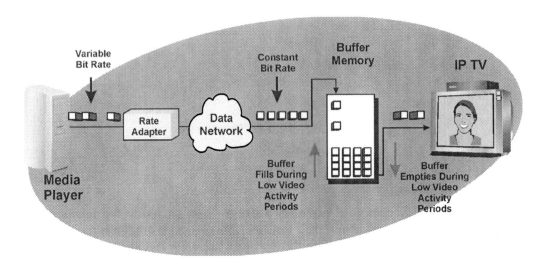

Figure 1.27., Packet Buffering

Digital Storage Media Command and Control (DSM-CC)

Digital storage media command and control is an MPEG extension that allows for the control of MPEG streaming. DSM-CC provides VCR type features.

Real Time Interface (RTI)

Real time interface is an extension to the MPEG system that defines an interface that allows the connection of devices to MPEG bit streams.

Media Synchronization

Media synchronization is the process of adjusting the relative timing of media information (such as time aligning audio and video media). Media synchronization typically involves sending timing references in each media stream that can be used to align and adjust the relative timing of multiple media signals.

Media synchronization is especially important for packet based systems that can have variable amounts of delay between media sources. The variable packet transmission time may result in media components being recreated (rendered) at different times.

To provide media synchronization in MPEG systems, a program clock reference (PCR) is used. A PCR is a reference source of timing information that is used as a reference to all the media streams associated with that program. The PCR is a 42-bit field that is transmitted at least every 100 msec.

Figure 1.28 shows how MPEG can be used to time synchronize multiple media channels with each other. This diagram shows that MPEG channels include program clock reference (PCR) time stamps to allow all of the elementary streams to remain time synchronized with each other.

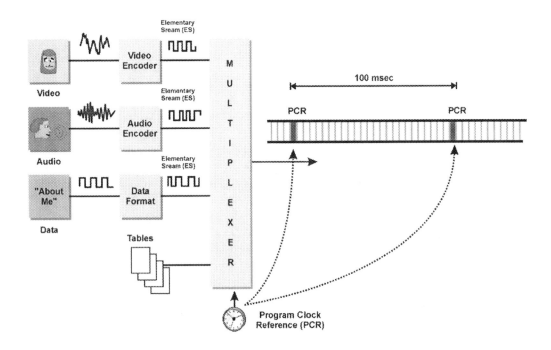

Figure 1.28., MPEG Media Synchronization

Display Formatting

Display formatting is the positioning and timing of graphic elements on a display area (such as on a television or computer display). Display formatting may combine mixed types media such as video, animation, graphics and interactive controls on a video or television monitor.

MPEG has several protocols that can be used to position and sequence the presentation of media. These protocols include synchronized multimedia integration language (SMIL), binary format for scenes (BIFS) and active format description (AFD).

SMIL is a protocol that is used to control the user interface with multimedia sessions. SMIL is used to setup and control the operation of media files along with the placement and operation windows on the user's display. Binary format for scenes is part of the MPEG-4 standard that deals with synchronizing video and audio. AFD is a set of commands that are sent on a video bit stream that describes key areas of interest in a video or image sequence. The use of AFD allows the receiver or set top boxes to adjust or optimize the display for a viewer.

Figure 1.29 shows how MPEG can use BIFS to position and coordinate the timing of media to different areas of a display. This example shows a television that has is displaying different types of media. In the top left, a video is streaming in the window area. To the top left, an image of a new game that has been released is shown. On the bottom, text is display with interactive buttons on the right of each text line.

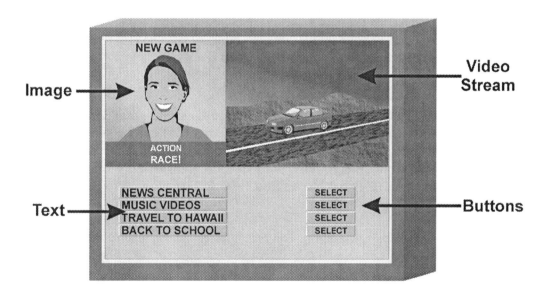

Figure 1.29., MPEG Display Formatting

Digital Video Quality (DVQ)

Digital video quality is the ability of a display or video transfer system to recreate the key characteristics of an original digital video signal. Digital video and transmission system impairments include tiling, error blocks, smearing, jerkiness, artifacts and object retention.

Video quality is subjective and cannot always be directly related to signal quality levels and the distortion that occurs on analog video that is different than the distortion that occurs on digital signals.

Tiling is the changing of a digital video image into square tiles that are located in positions other than their original positions on the screen. Error blocks are groups of image bits (a block of pixels) in a digital video signal that do not represent error signals rather than the original image bits that were supposed to be in that image block. Jerkiness is holding or skipping of video image frames or fields in a digital video. Visual artifacts are the unintended, unwanted visual aberrations in an image (such as blocks on a video image or speckles on a picture image around sharp edges). Object retention is the keeping of a portion of a frame or field on a digital video display when the image has changed.

Figure 1.30 shows some of the causes and effects of video distortion that may occur in IP Television systems. This example shows that video digitization and compression converts video into packets that can be sent through data networks (such as the Internet). Packet loss and packet corruption results in distorted video signals. This example shows that some types of distortion include tiling, error blocks and retained images.

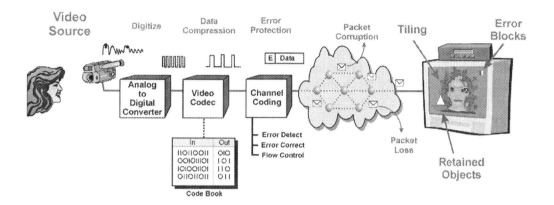

Figure 1.30., Digital Video Quality

Digital Rights Management (DRM)

Digital rights management is a system of access control and copy protection used to control the distribution of digital media. DRM involves the control of physical access to information, identity validation (authentication), service authorization, and media protection (encryption). DRM systems are typically incorporated or integrated with other systems such as content management system, billing systems, and royalty management. Some of the key parts of DRM systems include key management, product packaging, user rights management (URM), data encryption, product fulfillment and product monitoring. MPEG system defines how DRM system can be implemented in the MPEG-21 standard.

The MPEG system can transfer conditional access messages that enable the descrambling and decoding of media for one or more users of media. CAMs are composed of control messages, service keys and user keys. For the MPEG systems, there are two types of CAMs; entitlement control messages (ECM) and entitlement management messages (EMM).

Entitlement control messages are conditional access system commands commonly used in broadcast systems that contain access parameters and procedures. ECMs typically provide access and decoding information for short time periods (such as every 10 seconds). ECMs are sent continuously to allow the media stream to be decoded as encryption codes change.

Entitlement Management Messages are information elements that allow the encryption and/or decryption of information (such as a descrambling code for a digital television channel).

There are two types of keys used in an MPEG system; service keys and user keys. A service key is a code that is used to modify information or data for a particular service. A service key in an MPEG system is used to scramble control words. User keys are unique codes that are specific to each user or device.

There are two key options available to the MPEG system for DRM; simulcrypting and multicrypting. Simulcrypting is the simultaneous sending of encrypted signals to multiple devices (such as a cable set top box) where each receiver is provided with decryption codes. Multicrypt is the ability of one device (such as a cable set top box) to have or decode multiple encryption codes. Multicrypt systems can store and use information on smart cards to decode media for specific users.

Figure 1.31 shows how MPEG enables the use of conditional access and digital rights management systems. This example shows that the MPEG system may use a combination of user keys and service keys to scramble the MPEG signal. This example shows that the conditional access table (CAT) provides the PID for the EMM and the program map table (PMT) provides the PID for the EMC. The receiver uses these messages along with other information (such as the smart card) to descramble the MPEG signal.

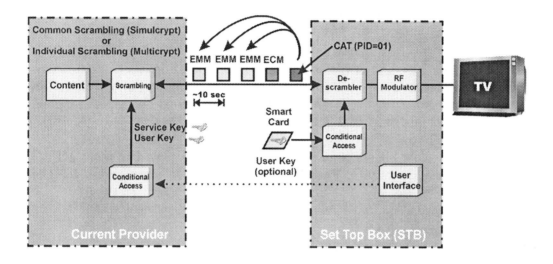

Figure 1.31., MPEG Digital Rights Management

MPEG-1

MPEG-1 is a multimedia transmission system that allows the combining and synchronizing of multiple media types (e.g. digital audio and digital video). MPEG-1 was primarily developed for CD-ROM multimedia applications. Because it is primarily focused on multimedia computers, there was no defined way to process interlaced video. The compression processes used in MPEG-1 systems can compress digital video up to 52 to 1.

Part 1 of the MPEG-1 specification defines the overall system operation. It explains how the audio and video streams are combined into a single data stream and how these streams are separated, decoded and time synchronized.

Part 2 defines how digital video is coded for compressing video sequences allowing bit rates up to 1.5 Mbps. This standard defines the use of spatial (image compression) and temporal (multiple sequences) through the use of image blocks and a prediction on how these blocks will move between frames.

Part 3 defines how audio is compressed. There are 3 levels of audio compression defined in part 3 ranging from the least complex (low compression ratio) to the most complex (highest compression ratio). The most complex, level 3 is the origin of MPEG-1, part 3 (MP3).

Part 4 defines how bit streams and decoders can be tested to meet MPEG specification requirements. Part 5 provides software simulations for the MPEG-1 system.

MPEG-2

MPEG-2 is a frame oriented multimedia transmission system that allows the combining and synchronizing of multiple media types. MPEG-2 is the current choice of video compression for digital television broadcasters as it can provide digital video quality that is similar to NTSC with a data rate of approximately 3.8 Mbps. The MPEG-2 system defines a digital video encoding process that can compress digital video up to 100 to 1.

The MPEG-2 system was developed to provide broadcast television applications so it has the ability to support progressive and interlaced video formats. The data rates for MPEG-2 systems can range from approximately 1.5 to 60 Mbps.

Part 1 of the MPEG-2 system provides overview that defines the media streams and how they are combined into programs. Part 2 describes how programs are combined onto transport streams that can be transmitted over satellite, broadcast television and cable TV networks.

Part 3 defines the how multiple channel audio can be transmitted on MPEG. The MPEG-2 audio system allows more than 2 channels of audio permitting surround sound applications. Part 4 defines how bit streams and decoders can be tested to meet MPEG specification requirements.

Part 5 provides software simulations for the MPEG-2 system. Part 6 defines the protocols that can provide media flow commands that can be used by users to start, pause and stop the play of media.

Part 7 describes the more efficient advanced audio codec (AAC) which is not backward compatible with previous MPEG audio coding systems. Part 8 was created to define how video coding could use 10 bit samples. This development of this part was discontinued.

Part 9 describes how a real interface (RTI) could be used to allow stream decoders to connect to transport streams. Part 10 contains conformance-testing processes for DSM-CC.

MPEG-4

MPEG-4 is a digital multimedia transmission standard that was designed to allow for interactive digital television and it can have more efficient compression capability than MPEG-2 (more than 200:1 compression).

A Key feature of MPEG-4 is its ability to manage separate media components within image frames. These media objects can be independently controlled and compressed more efficiently. MPEG-4 can model media components into 2 dimensional or 3 dimensional scenes. It has the ability to sense and adjust the delivery of media dependent on the media channel type such as fairly reliable broadcast or unreliable Internet.

The overall structure and operation MPEG-4 system is described in Part 1. Part 2 defines the original video compression codec that was used in the MPEG-4 system. While this video codec offered an improvement in compression (a small amount) over the MPEG-2 video compression process, it was a relatively small improvement. Part 3 contains a set of audio codecs along with speech coding tools.

Part 4 defines the testing and conformance processes that are used to ensure devices meet the MPEG specifications. Part 5 contains reference software that can be used to demonstrate or test the operation of the MPEG-4 system.

Part 6 provides the delivery multimedia integration framework (DMIF) structure that allows a multimedia system (such as MPEG) to identify the sources of media and the transmission characters for that media source (such as from a high bandwidth low error rate DVD or through a limited bandwidth mobile telephone system). The use of DMIF allows the playback system to become independent from the sources and their transmission limitations.

Part 7 contains reference software that can be used to optimize MPEG systems. Part 8 describes how to send MPEG signals through IP networks. Part 9 provides reference hardware designs that can be used to demonstrate how to implement MPEG solutions.

Part 10 is the advanced video coding/H.264 part that provides substantial compression improvements over the MPEG-2 video compression system. Part 11 contains the binary format for scenes part of the MPEG-4 standard, which deals with synchronizing video and audio. Part 12 describes the file format that can be used for storing the media components of a program.

Part 13 contains the intellectual property management and protection protocol that is used in the MPEG system to enable digital rights management (DRM). Part 14 defines the container file format that can be used for MPEG-4 files. Part 15 defines the file format that can be used to store video that is compressed using the advanced video coder (AVC).

Part 16 contains the animation framework extension (AFX) set of 3D tools for interactive 3D content operating at the geometry, modeling and biomechanical level. Part 17 defines how text subtitles can be combined and timed with MPEG media. Part 18 defines how fonts can be compressed and streamed. Part 19 describes how to provide synthesized texture streams.

MPEG-7

MPEG-7 is a system that can be used to describe the characteristics and related information about digital media objects. The MPEG-7 system is an XML based language. The MPEG-7 system uses description definition language (DDL) to describe the characteristic objects using existing (standard) and custom created definitions. Some of the standard characteristics include shape, texture and motion.

Part 1 of MPEG-7 is an overview of the key tools that are needed to describe media objects in MPEG systems. Part 2 provides the description definition language (DDL) that defines the syntax of the MPEG descriptions and how to extend (create) custom description. Part 3 explains the tools that cover visual descriptions. Part 4 explains the tools that cover audio descriptions.

Part 5 defines how to develop multimedia descriptions for objects with generic features. Part 6 contains reference software that can be used to demonstrate and test MPEG-7 systems. Part 7 provides the processes that allow testing to ensure products and software meet the requirements of the MPEG-7 system. Part 8 covers the extraction and use of descriptions. Part 9 contains the profiles and levels for MPEG-7. Part 10 describes the structure (schema) of the description definition language (DDL).

MPEG-21

MPEG-21 is a multimedia specification that adds digital rights management capability to MPEG systems. MPEG-21 is an architecture that enables the searching, selecting, defining and managing the rights associated with digital media objects.

The MPEG-21 standard parts include digital item declaration (DID), digital item identification (DII), intellectual property management and protection (IPMP), rights expression language (REL), rights data dictionary (RDD) and digital item adaptation (DIA).

Part 2 defines digital the common set of terms and descriptions that can define a digital media object. Part 3 explains digital item identification (DII) can uniquely identify any type or portion of content. Part 4 describes the intellectual property management and protection is a protocol that is used in the MPEG system to enable digital rights management (DRM).

Part 5 defines how rights expression language (REL) protocol can be used to specify rights to content along with fees or other consideration required to secure those rights. Part 6 contains the rights data dictionary (RDD).

Part 7 covers digital item adaptation (DIA) which defines the semantics and syntax that may be used to adapt the format or transmission of digital items. Part 8 provides reference software that can be used to demonstrate or test the operation of the MPEG-21 system. Part 9 describes file formats.

MPEG Profiles

MPEG profiles are a particular implementation or set of required protocols and actions that enables the providing of features and services for particular MPEG applications. These applications range from providing standard television services over a broadcast system to providing video services on a mobile wireless network. The use of profiles allows an MPEG device or service to only use or include the necessary capabilities (such as codec types) that are required to deliver media to the applications.

Profiles are created for specific applications and types of media. New profiles are constantly being requested and created. Because the types of applications of applications that use MPEG transmission can dramatically vary, MPEG has tens of profiles and there are different profile types for the MPEG-2 and MPEG-4 systems.

MPEG-2 Profiles

MPEG-2 profiles include simple profiles (low complexity), main (standard TV), scalable profile (variable capabilities), high profile (HDTV), and 4:2:2 profile (studio quality).

Simple Profile (SP)

The simple MPEG profile provides video for relatively simple bandwidth limited devices such as mobile telephones and personal digital assistants. The simple profile does not allow the use of bi-directional frames (B-Frames) which keeps the coding complexity low.

Main Profile (MP)

Main profile is a common set of protocols and processes that are used to provide standard television services. The main profile used in the MPEG system allows for the use of Intra frames (I-Frames), predicted frames (P-Frames) and bi-directional frames (B-Frames). The MPEG main profile also allows for the use of interlacing The main profile is commonly used for broadcast television applications.

Scalable Profile

Scalable profile is the set of MPEG protocols and processes that can provide video with varying bandwidth and performance needs. The scalable profile defines a base layer along with layers that are used to enhance the quality or performance of a video signal. The scalable profile enables the use of mobile devices that have varying capabilities of reception and display resolution.

High Profile (HP)

High profile is the set of MPEG protocols and processes that are used for high definition television (HDTV). Although the high profile was originally developed for HDTV service, the main profile levels were expanded to enable the transmission of HDTV signals using the main profile.

4:2:2 Profile

4:2:2 profile is a set of protocols and process that are used to provide high quality color video for studio production and distribution services. The 4:2:2 contains more color elements than the standard 4:2:0 YUV color format. The 4:2:2 profile allows for the use of I-frames, P-frames and B-frames. At standard resolution (720x576), its maximum data rate is 50 Mbps and at high definition (1920x1080), the maximum data rate is 300 Mbps.

Figure 1.32 shows the different types of profiles and how they are used in the MPEG-2 systems. This table shows that the key MPEG-2 profile types include simple, main, scalable, high and 4:2:2 studio profiles. Simple profiles are used for low complexity devices (such as portable media players). The main profile is used for standard broadcast television applications. Scalable profiles offer the ability to provide varying levels of service different types of devices (such as wireless devices). The high profile is used for high definition television. The 4:2:2 profile is used for studio production and distribution.

Profile	Typical Use
Simple Profile	Portable Media Players (low complexity)
Main Profile	Standard Television
Scalable Profile	Wireless Media Devices
High Profile	High Definition TV (HDTV)
4:2:2	Studio Production

Figure 1.32., MPEG-2 Profile Types

MPEG-4 Profiles

MPEG-4 profiles include audio profiles, visual profiles, MPEG-J profiles (application programming interfaces), advanced video coding (higher compression), scene distribution (dimensional control) and graphics profiles (image processing).

Audio Profiles

Audio profiles are protocols and processes that are used to provide audio transfer and rendering applications and services. The audio profiles focus on specific applications that require tradeoffs such as the tradeoff of having a high audio compression ratio which results in increased audio processing (coding time) delays and higher sensitivity to transmission errors. Additional tradeoffs include speech coding (optimized for human voice) that can offer a high compression ratio as opposed to natural audio coding with relatively low compression ratios that can reproduce any sound.

The MPEG-4 system has several audio profiles including speech profile, synthesis profile, scalable profile, main profile, high quality audio profile, low delay audio profile, natural audio profile and mobile audio internetworking profile.

The speech profile can be used to produce a range of speech audio functions ranging from high bit rate waveform coding to very low bit rate text to speech audio coding. Text to speech conversion transforms text (ASCII) information into synthetic speech output. This technology is used in voice processing applications that require the production of broad, unrelated and unpredictable vocabularies (e.g., products in a catalog, names and addresses, etc.).

Synthesis profile defines how the MPEG system can use wave table synthesis and text to speech to create audio. The scalable profile can use different bit rates and audio bandwidths to effectively provide audio that contains music and speech. Main profile contains tools for natural and synthetic audio.

High quality audio profile allows for the use of advanced audio coding (AAC) which is more efficient (has a higher data compression ratio) than the MP3 coder. The low delay audio profile uses speech coders and text to speech interfaces to provide low delay real time communication. It is a version of the advanced audio coder that reduces the amount of processing time for coding which can be used for real time two-way communication applications.

Natural audio profile contains the capabilities for natural (non-synthetic) audio coding. Mobile audio internetworking profile uses a scalable AAC with low delay to enable high quality audio coding processes for time sensitive applications (such as video conferencing).

Visual Profiles

Visual profiles are protocols and processes that are used to provide video transfer and rendering services. The MPEG-4 system video profiles have capabilities that include the transfer of arbitrarily shaped objects (as opposed to rectangular shaped objects), scalable (variable quality) images, layered (images that can be enhanced) and the transfer and remote (local creation) of animated images.

Simple visual profile is a low complexity video coding system that can be used for portable video devices such as multimedia cellular telephones. Because it is a simple profile, it does not include the ability to provide interlaced video.

Simple scalable visual profile can carry over multiple sequences (temporal scalability) or over multiple areas (spatial scalability) to allow operation at different bit rates.

The fine granularity scalability profile has the ability to layer multiple levels of image quality. It starts with a base layer and ads enhancement layers to improve the resolution of the images. It can be used in systems to offer different quality levels when bandwidth is selectable or adjustable.

Advanced simple profile (ASP) can use B-frames and can use $1/4^{th}$ pel compensation to increase the compression ratio (it is approximately $1/3^{rd}$ more efficient than simple visual profile). Core visual profile has the ability to define objects that have different (arbitrary) shapes. It is useful for applications that have interactivity between media objects. The core scalable profile includes improved scalability options for arbitrarily shaped objects.

Main visual profile includes the ability to process interlaced video objects. The main visual profile can be used for broadcast and interactive DVD applications.

N-bit visual profile defines how to code video objects using pixel depths that range from 4 bits to 12 bits. Advanced core profile includes the ability to process arbitrarily shaped video and still images.

Advance coding efficiency profile (ACE) adds tools that can increase the compression ratio for both rectangular and arbitrarily shaped video objects.

Simple studio profile is used to maintain the quality of video for studio distribution and editing functions. The studio simple only uses I frames. The core studio profile ads P-frames to the simple studio profile allowing a higher compression ratio at the expense of added complexity.

The simple facial animation visual profile uses a mathematical model to animate facial images. This allows for the sending of a very small amount of data (e.g. lips move a small amount) to create 3 dimensional images. The simple face and body animation profile uses a mathematical model to animate both facial and body images.

Advanced real time simple (ARTS) uses a low delay coding process along with robust error coding to provide real time two-way communication that cannot tolerate delays and which are subject to high error rates.

The scalable texture visual profile allows for the mapping of textures onto images. Basic animated 2D texture visual profile has the capability to insert textures onto 2D images. Advanced scalable texture profile can perform scalable shape coding. This includes wavelet tiling.

The hybrid visual profile includes the capability to decode synthetic and natural objects.

Advanced Video Coding Profiles

Advanced video coding profiles are protocols and processes that are used to provide advanced video transfer and rendering capabilities to underlying MPEG services. The AVC profiles use the H.264/AVC coder that provides a compression ratio that is approximately double the MPEG-2 video coder. The AVC profiles range from low complexity baseline profile (BP) to an ultra high professional quality 4:4:4 profile.

The baseline profile (BP) is used for low complexity device such as portable media players. Extended profile (XP) is designed for streaming video over networks that may have high packet loss (such as the Internet).

The main profile was designed for broadcast (e.g. Cable TV) and storage (e.g. DVD) applications. High profile (HiP) can provide high definition television for broadcast and stored media distribution systems. High 10 profile (Hi10P) provides for increased quality allowing up to 10 bits per sample of decoded picture elements.

High 4:2:2 profile (Hi422P) is used for professional applications that require higher levels of chroma (color) elements. High 4:4:4 profile (Hi422P) adds additional chroma (color) elements and allows up to 12 bits per image element.

MPEG-J Profiles

MPEG-J profiles are protocols and processes that are used to provide application programming interface (API) capabilities to underlying MPEG services. The MPEG-4 system has several MPEG-J profiles including personal profile and main profile.

Personal MPEG-J profile is used for low complexity portable devices such as gaming devices, mobile telephones and portable media players. Main MPEG-J profile includes all the profiles from personal MPEG-J profiles plus APIs that can be used to select and configuring decoders along with interfaces to access service information.

Scene Graph Profiles

Scene graph profiles are the sets of protocols and processes that are used to define a composite (mixture) of media objects and how they relate to each other in an area. Scene graph profiles can be used to define the hierarchical relationship between videos, graphic images and audio components in a 2 dimensional or 3 dimensional enviornment.

Some of the scene graphs profiles are based on the virtual reality modeling language (VRML) protocol. VRML is a text based language that is used to allow the creation of three-dimensional viewpoints, primarily for use with Web browsing.

The MPEG-4 system scene graph profiles include the basic 2D profile, simple 2D scene graph profile, complete 2D scene graph profile, core 2D profile, advanced 2D profile, main 2D profile, X3D profile, complete scene graph profile, audio scene graph proifle and 3D audio scene graph profile.

The basic 2D profile is used to define simple scenes on a 2 dimensional area. It is used for audio only or video only applications. The simple 2D scene graph profile can place media objects into a scene on a 2 dimensional area. It is a low complexity profile and it and does not define interaction with the media objects. Complete 2D scene graph profile allows for alpha blending and interactivity with the media objects. Alpha blending is the combining of a translucent foreground color with a background color to produce a new blended color.

The core 2D profile can use both audio and visual media objects. It allows for local animation and interaction. Local animation is a process that changes parameters or features of an image or object over time that is processed at the location where the animation is playing (e.g. within a television or multimedia computer).

The advanced 2D profile contains the capabilities of the basic 2D and core 2D profiles along with adding scripting capability and local interaction.

The main 2D profile ads FlexeTime model which allows input sensors and additional tools for interactive applications. It is designed to interoperate with synchronized multimedia integration language (SMIL). SMIL is a protocol that is used to control the user interface with multimedia sessions. SMIL is used to setup and control the operation of media files along with the placement and operation windows on the users display.

The X3D profile is a small footprint (limited memory and processing requirements) 3 dimensional media processing profile. It is designed to interoperate with X3D specification created by the Web3D consortium. Extensible 3D (X3D) is a storage, retreival and rendering (playback) industry standard for real time graphics media objects which can be adjusted in relative position and possibly interact with each other.

Complete scene graph profile is a combined set of 2D and 3D scene graph profiles from the binary format for scenes (BIFS) toolbox. Complete scene graph profile can be used for vitual gaming that have 3 dimensional worlds.

Audio scene graph profile is used for applications that only require audio media. The 3D audio scene graph profile describes how to position sound in a 3 dimensional environment. It allows for interaction of sounds with objects within the scene.

Graphics Profiles

Graphics profiles are sets of protocols and processes that are used to define and control graphics elements that are used in scenes. Some of the graphics profiles used in MPEG-4 systems include simple 2D graphics profile, simple 2D + text profile, core 2D profile, advanced 2D profile, complete 2D graphics profile, comlete graphics profile, 3D audio graphics profile, and X3D core profile.

The simple 2D graphics profile is used for placing media objects in a scene that has only 2 dimensions. The simple 2D + text profile adds the ability to include text on the screen and to allow the text to move and be transformed (e.g. become transparent) with other media objects.

Core 2D profile is used for picture in picture (PIP), video warping, animated advertisements and logo insertion. The advanced 2D profile adds graphic user interface (GUI) capabilities along with more complex graphics control for animation.

Complete 2D graphics profile is a full set of 2D graphics control capabilities including the use of multiple shaped graphic objects. The complete graphics profile allows for the use of elevation grids, extrusions and lighitng effects to create virtual worlds.

3D audio graphics profile is used to define the acoustical properties of a scene. It includes features such as acoustics absorption, acoustic diffusion, acoustic transparency and tele-presence.

The X3D core profile includes 3 dimenstional media object processing capabilities for advanced gaming and virtual environments. It is compatible with X3D specification.

Figure 1.33 shows the different types of profiles used in the MPEG-4 systems. This table shows that the key MPEG-4 profile types include audio, visual, advanced video, MPEG-J, scenes and graphics profiles. The audio profiles range from very low bit rate to high quality audio that can be used in cinemas. The visual profiles range from low resolution profiles that can be used in portable devices to high quality studio profiles. Advanced video coding profiles take advantage of the high compression AVC coder. MPEG-J profiles allow the device to have direct programming interfaces to the MPEG media and devices. Scenes profiles define the relationships between media objects. Graphics profiles define media objects and how they are positioned on displays and how they can be changed in scenes.

Profile Type	Profile Uses
Audio	Audio Media Players (from simple audio only to digital cinema)
Visual	Various Levels of Video Support (from variable resolution to studio quality)
Advanced Video Coding	Various Levels of Video Support using Advanced (high compression) Video Coder
MPEG-J (Java)	Application Programming Interfaces
Scenes	Relationships between Media Objects (2D and 3D Scenes)
Graphics	Definition of the Graphics Elements used in Scenes

Figure 1.33., MPEG-4 Profile Types

MPEG Levels

MPEG levels are the amount of capability that a MPEG profile can offer. The use of levels allows products to define their quantitative capabilities such as memory size, resolution and maximum bit rates. For example, MPEG levels can range from low detail (low resolution) to very high capability (high resolution).

Low level MPEG signals have a resolution format of up to 360 x 288 (SIF). Main level MPEG signals provide for resolution of up to 720x576 (standard definition television). High level can support resolution of up to 1920x1152 (high definition). One of the more common profile combinations is the main profile at the main level (MP@ML). This combination provides television signals for standard definition (SD).

Figure 1.34 shows the different levels used in the MPEG-2 system. This table shows that low level has low resolution capability with a maximum bit rate of 4 Mbps. The main level has standard definition (SD) capability with a maximum bit rate of 15 Mbps. The high 1440 profile is a high definition format that has a maximum bit rate of 60 Mbps. The high level profile has a high definition format with 1152 lines that have 1920 pixels per line which can have a bit rate of up to 80 Mbps.

Name	Lines	Pixels per Line	Bitrate (Mbps)
Low Level (LL)	352	288	4
Main Level (ML)	576	720	15
High-1440 (H-14)	1152	1440	60
High Level (HL)	1152	1920	80

Figure 1.34., MPEG-2 Levels

Conformance Points

Conformance points are a combination of profiles and levels in a system (such as an MPEG system) where different products can interoperate (by conforming to that level and profile). An example of conformance points is if ability of a mobile video server to support creation and playback of a simple visual profile at level 0, any mobile phone that has these conformance points should be able to play a video with these profiles and levels.

Appendix 1

Acronyms

AAC-Advanced Audio Codec
AF-Adaptation Field
API-Application Program Interface
ASK-Amplitude Shift Keying
ATSC-Advanced Television Systems Committee
AU-Access Unit
AVC-Advanced Video Coding
BAT-Banquet Association Table
b-Bidirectional
BER-Bit Error Rate
BPSK-Binary Phase-Shift Keying
CA-Conditional Access
CAM-Conditional Access Message
CAT-Conditional Access Table
CCIR-Comite' Consultatif International de Radiocommunications
CCITT-Comite Consultatif International du Telegraphe at du Telephone
CD-Compact Disc
CIF-Common Interchange Format
CNR-Carrier To Noise Ratio
Codec-Coder/Decoder
COFDM-Coded Orthogonal Frequency Division Modulation
CSA-Common Scrambling Algorithm
CVBS-Comosite Video Baseband Signal
DAB-Digital Audio Broadcast
DAC-Digital To Analog Converter
DAVIC-Digital Audio Video Council
DC-Direct Current

DCT-Discrete Cosine Transform
DiSEqC-Digital Satellite Equipment Control
DOCSIS-Data Over Cable Service Interface Specifications
DPCM-Differential Pulse Code Modulation
DRAM-Dynamic Random Access Memory
DSM-CC-Digital Storage Media Command and Control
DSM-Digital Storage Media
DSP-Digital Signal Processor
DSS-Digital Satellite Systems
DTS-Decode Time Stamp
DTS-Decoding Time Stamp
DVB-CI-Digital Video Broadcasting Common Interface
DVB-Digital Video Broadcasting
DVB-SI-Digital Video Broadcasting Service Information
dvd-Digital Versatile Disk
DVQ-Digital Video Quality
EBU-European Broadcasting Union
ECM-Entitlement Control Messages
EI-Error Indication
EIT-Event Information Table
ELG-European Launching Group
EMM-Entitlement Management Messages
EPG-Electronic Programming Guide

ES-Elementary Stream
ETSI-European Telecommunications Standards Institute
FCC-Federal Communications Commission
FEC-Forward Error Correction
FFT-Fast Fourier Transform
FIFO-First-In-First-Out
FSK-Frequency Shift Keying
FSS-Fixed Satellite Service
FTA-Free to Air
GOP-Group of Pictures
HD-High Definition
HDMI-High Definition Multimedia Interface
HDTV-High Definition Television
HE AAC-High Efficiency Advanced Audio Codec
HTML-Hypertext Markup Language
IDTV-Improved Definition Television
iDTV-Integrated Digital Television Receiver
IEC-International Electrotechnical Commission
I-In-Phase
I-Intra
IRD-Integrated Receiver and Decoder
ISDB-T-Integrated Services Digital Broadcasting Terrestrial
ISI-Inter Symbol Interference
ISO-International Standards Organization
ITU-International Telecommunication Union
JPEG-Joint Photographic Experts Group
LNC-Low Noise Converter
MAC-Medium Access Control
MHEG5-Multimedia and Hypermedia Expert Group Version 5
MHP-Multimedia Home Platform
MP@ML-Main Profile at Main Level
MP3-Motion Picture Experts Group Layer 3
MPEG-Motion Picture Experts Group

MPEG-TS-MPEG transport stream
MUSICAM-Masking Universal Sub-band Intergrated Coding and Multiplexing
NICAM-Near Instantaneous Companded Audio Multiplexing
NIT-Network Information Table
NTSC-National Television System Committee
OFDM-Orthogonal Frequency Division Multiplexing
OOB-Out of band
PAL ID-PAL Identification
PAL-Phase Alternating Line
PAT-Program Allocating Table
PAT-programs in a transport channel
PCM-Pulse Coded Modulation
PCR-Program Clock Reference
PES-Packet Elementary Stream
PES-Packetized Elementary Stream
PID-packet identification code
PID-Packet Identifier
PMT-Program Map Table
p-Predictive Frames
PRBS-Pseudo-Random Binary Sequence
PSI-Program Specific Information
PS-Program Stream
PTS-Presentation Time Stamp
PU-Presentation Unit
PUSI-Payload Unit Start Indicator
QAM-Quadrature Amplitude Modulation
QCIF-Quarter Common Intermediate Format
QEF-Quasi Error Free
QPSK-Quadrature Phase Shift Keying
Q-Quadrature
RISC-Reduced Instruction Set Computer
RLC-Run Length Coding
RST-Running Status Table
RTI-Real Time Interface
SCR-System Clock Reference
SDRAM-Synchronous Dynamic Random Access Memory

SD-Standard Definition
SDT-Service Description Table
SECAM-Sequential Couleur Avec
MeMoire
SFN-Single Frequency Network
SIF-Source Intermediate Format
SMIL-Synchronized Multimedia
Integration Language
SPTS-Single Program Transport Stream
STC-System Time Clock
STD-System Target Decoder
STS-system time stamp
ST-Stuffing Table
TDT-Time and Date Table
TPS-Transmission Parameter Signaling
URM-User Rights Management
USB-Universal Serial Bus
VBS-Video Baseband Signal
VLC-Variable Length Coding
VLIW-Very Long Instruction Word
VSB-Vestigial Sideband
WSS-Wide Screeen Signaling

Index

Althos Publishing Book List
Winter 2005-06

Product ID	Title	# Pages	ISBN	Price	Copyright
Billing					
BK7727874	Introduction to Telecom Billing	48	0974278742	$11.99	2004
BK7769438	Introduction to Wireless Billing	44	097469438X	$14.99	2004
Business					
BK7781359	How to Get Private Business Loans	56	1932813594	$14.99	2005
BK7781368	Career Coach	92	1932813683	$14.99	2006
Datacom					
BK7727873	Introduction to Data Networks	48	0974278734	$11.99	2003
IP Telephony					
BK7727877	Introduction to IP Telephony	80	0974278777	$12.99	2003
BK7781361	Tehrani's IP Telephony Dictionary, 2nd Edition	628	1932813616	$39.99	2005
BK7780530	Internet Telephone Basics	224	0972805303	$29.99	2003
BK7780532	Voice over Data Networks for Managers	348	097280532X	$49.99	2003
BK7780538	Introduction to SIP IP Telephony Systems	144	0972805389	$14.99	2003
BK7781311	Creating RFPs for IP Telephony Communication Systems	86	193281311X	$19.99	2004
BK7781309	IP Telephony Basics	324	1932813098	$34.99	2004
BK7769430	Introduction to SS7 and IP	56	0974694304	$12.99	2004
IP Television					
BK7781362	Creating RFPs for IP Television Systems	86	1932813624	$19.99	2005
BK7781357	IP Television Directory	154	1932813578	$89.99	2005
BK7781355	Introduction to Data Multicasting	68	1932813551	$14.99	2005
BK7781340	Introduction to Digital Rights Management (DRM)	84	1932813403	$14.99	2005
BK7781351	Introduction to IP Audio	64	1932813519	$14.99	2005
BK7781335	Introduction to IP Television	104	1932813357	$14.99	2005
BK7781330	Introduction to IP Video Servers	68	1932813306	$14.99	2005
BK7781341	Introduction to IP Video	88	1932813411	$14.99	2005
BK7781352	Introduction to Mobile Video	68	1932813527	$14.99	2005
BK7781353	Introduction to MPEG	72	1932813535	$14.99	2005
BK7781342	Introduction to Premises Distribution Networks (PDN)	68	193281342X	$14.99	2005
BK7781354	Introduction to Telephone Company Television (Telco TV)	84	1932813543	$14.99	2005
BK7781344	Introduction to Video on Demand (VOD)	68	1932813446	$14.99	2005
BK7781356	IP Television Basics	308	193281356X	$34.99	2005
BK7781334	IP TV Dictionary	652	1932813349	$39.99	2005
BK7781363	IP Video Basics	280	1932813632	$34.99	2005
Programming					
BK7727875	Wireless Markup Language (WML)	287	0974278750	$34.99	2003
BK7781300	Introduction to xHTML:	58	1932813004	$14.99	2004
Legal and Regulatory					
BK7769433	Practical Patent Strategies Used by Successful Companies	48	0974694339	$14.99	2003
BK7781332	Strategic Patent Planning for Software Companies	58	1932813322	$14.99	2004
BK7780533	Patent or Perish	220	0972805338	$39.95	2003
Telecom					
BK7727872	Introduction to Private Telephone Systems 2nd Edition	86	0974278726	$14.99	2005
BK7727876	Introduction to Public Switched Telephone 2nd Edition	54	0974278769	$14.99	2005
BK7780537	SS7 Basics, 3rd Edition	276	0972805370	$34.99	2003
BK7780535	Telecom Basics, 3rd Edition	354	0972805354	$29.99	2003
BK7727870	Introduction to Transmission Systems	52	097427870X	$14.99	2004
BK7781313	ATM Basics	156	1932813136	$29.99	2004
BK7781302	Introduction to SS7	138	1932813020	$19.99	2004
BK7781345	Introduction to Digital Subscriber Line (DSL)	72	1932813454	$14.99	2005

For a complete list please visit
www.AlthosBooks.com

ALTHOS

Althos Publishing Book List
Winter 2005-06

Wireless

Product ID	Title	Pages	ISBN	Price	Year
BK7781306	Introduction to GPRS and EDGE	98	1932813063	$14.99	2004
BK7781304	Introduction to GSM	110	1932813047	$14.99	2004
BK7727878	Introduction to Satellite Systems	72	0974278785	$14.99	2005
BK7727879	Introduction to Wireless Systems	536	0974278793	$11.99	2003
BK7769432	Introduction to Mobile Telephone Systems	48	0974694320	$10.99	2003
BK7769435	Introduction to Bluetooth	60	0974694355	$14.99	2004
BK7769436	Introduction to Private Land Mobile Radio	50	0974694363	$14.99	2004
BK7769434	Introduction to 802.11 Wireless LAN (WLAN)	62	0974694347	$14.99	2004
BK7769437	Introduction to Paging Systems	42	0974694371	$14.99	2004
BK7781308	Introduction to EVDO	84	193281308X	$14.99	2004
BK7781305	Introduction to Code Division Multiple Access (CDMA)	100	1932813055	$14.99	2004
BK7781303	Wireless Technology Basics	50	1932813039	$12.99	2004
BK7781312	Introduction to WCDMA	112	1932813128	$14.99	2004
BK7780534	Wireless Systems	536	0972805346	$34.99	2004
BK7769431	Wireless Dictionary	670	0974694312	$39.99	2005
BK7769439	Introduction to Mobile Data	62	0974694398	$14.99	2005

Optical

Product ID	Title	Pages	ISBN	Price	Year
BK7781329	Introduction to Optical Communication	132	1932813292	$14.99	2006

Order Form

Phone: 1 919-557-2260
Fax: 1 919-557-2261   Date:_____
404 Wake Chapel Rd., Fuquay-Varina, NC 27526 USA

Name:_____ Title:_____
Company:_____
Shipping Address:_____
City:_____ State:_____ Postal/ Zip:_____
Billing Address:_____
City:_____ State:_____ Postal/ Zip _____
Telephone:_____ Fax:_____
Email: _____
Payment (select): VISA ___ AMEX ___ MC ___ Check ____
Credit Card #: _____Expiration Date: _____
Exact Name on Card: _____

Qty.	Product ID	ISBN	Title	Price Ea	Total
Book Total:					
Sales Tax (North Carolina Residents please add 7% sales tax)					
Shipping: $5 per book in the USA, $10 per book outside USA (most countries). Lower shipping and rates may be available online.					
Total order:					

For a complete list please visit
www.AlthosBooks.com